OVERCOMER

31 DAY DEVOTIONAL FOR OVERCOMING
ADVERSITY, DEPRESSION, REJECTION,
TEMPTATION

CHESMA C. MCCOY

PUBLISHING

Shirley LaTour, shirley@shirleylatourenterprises.com

Or Chesma McCoy at www.pastorscloset.org

Publisher: SL Elite Publishing

451-D East Central Texas Expy

Suite 276

Harker Heights, TX 76548

Overcomer may be purchased at special quantity discounts. Resale opportunities are available for donor programs, fund raising, book clubs, or other educational purposes for schools and universities. For more information contact: Shirley LaTour shirley@ shirleylatourenterprises.com or slelitepublishing.com

ISBN (Paperback): 978-1-950289-20-2
ISBN (EBook): 978-1-950289-21-9

www.slelitepublishing.com

CONTENTS

DEDICATION

*I dedicate this book to my Madea, Tommie Lee Brown (
deceased), my sister, Elicia Crathers, (deceased), my niece,
Ty'esha Taylor (deceased), and to the Pastors and Christian
leaders who lost their lives to suicide and depression;
although your LIFE was cut too soon BUT GOD's Will
shall prevail, and also to my legal guardians and my
extended family. I am truly grateful to God for every one of
you as you serve as a LIFE line extension of who I am today!
Love ya'll to LIFE!*

ACKNOWLEDGMENTS

Not that I have already obtained all this, or have already arrived at my goal, but I press on to take a hold of that which Christ Jesus has set forth. Brothers and sisters, I do not consider myself yet have taken hold of it. But one thing I do: Forgetting what is behind and pressing toward what is ahead, I press toward the goal to win the prize for which God has called me heavenward in Christ Jesus.
(Philippians 3:12-14)

I pray the manuscript in this book is received in good faith, good health and good spirits. I am just so grateful to God to be a part of the Kingdom and to serve His people. My heart is overjoyed in abundance. Thank you all for your love, prayers and support. I pray you all enjoy it!

To my husband, partner, and friend, Leonard, I am so grateful for you. Your love and support mean the most. I thank God for all our strengths and struggles because without them none of this effort will ever be made possible. We are not perfect by any means so we learn as we grow. I thank God for our family. Love you to LIFE! #forbetter

To my son, Cheston, my first-born, I am leaving to you a legacy. It is my prayer that you will soon discover your purpose. Never be afraid of failure or rejection. Always believe in yourself. Remember, to keep God first and you will never be last. Mom loves you more than you will ever know!

To my daughter, Leandra, my favorite girl, even though you are probably too young to read this now but always know your value and worth. Never allow anyone to validate you as a person. Let God be your vindicator. Walk with God everywhere you go. Let your beauty and light SHINE bright for HIS Glory! Mom loves you more than you will ever know!

To my mother, Gayle, you will always be my number one from day one, from the womb to the world; your love for me broke the mold. Even when no one else believed in me, YOU DID! I thank God chose you to be my mother. You are a TRUE WOMAN of STRENGTH! God bless and keep you!

To my father, Arnold, I am so thankful to God to be a part of your legacy and offspring that you bring!

Without you, there will be no me. I pray I make you proud.

To my legal guardians, James and Girtie Crathers, you are the real MVP! I thank God for your tutelage and accepting me as a part of your family. You set the stage to my spiritual maturity of Christ's foundation!

To my mother in love, Agnes, I thank God for our relationship. It is a blessing to be a part of your family!

To my sisters, Vanessa, Valancia (Roxanne), Debora, Joyce, Jamie, Andrea (Kay), Erika, Beinka, Rhoda, Latarsha, you are my first friends. You know they say that sisters help build each other up. I can attest that this is true. If ever I'm in trouble I know you would be the first to pull up. Thanks for always having my back. Love you to LIFE!!!

To my brothers, Ira, (Bird), Carlos and Nathaniel, Lawrence (Dynamite), Larry, Raymond, Anthony (Tony), you have some big shoes to fill. You are the head and not the tail. Never be afraid to take the lead. Remember to walk TALL when you are walking with God! You are our living legacy!

To my nieces, Felicia, LaTisha, Mia, Kymisha, Keiambra, Ciarra, Daysha, Analicia, Cecily, and Christiana, never allow anyone to define you as a person. Know your worth! Beauty is in the eye of the beholder. You can do anything you set your mind on just keep your mind stayed on Him!

To my nephews, Eric, Dawan, Paul (PJ), Marqveis, Tyrese, James, Jaleel, Donovan, Zykieth, Shamar, Jeremiah, you are the future. Never forget who you are. You are the head and not the tail. Follow the example of your ancestors. Keep God first and you will never be last!

To my great nieces and nephews, Darien (DJ), Mariah, Milani, Ariya, Avyah, D'Aundre, Destynie, Jayden, Mya, Deonte, Carlos Jr, and Jalik, you're never too young to start dreaming so always know that there's no dream too small to be ever be accomplished. If you can dream it, you will achieve it. Just believe it and you receive it! Have FAITH in God because He is the one with the master plan!

To my sista friends, Rhonda and Dawnyelle, there are not many people I can call friends but you hold that title with honor and I thank God for you. Thank you for being a shoulder! Love you like a sista!

To my brother friends, Oris and Dusty, my brothers from another mother, I admire your strength, wisdom and humility. You bring so much joy and inspiration to the kingdom. It's a blessing to call you friend! Love you! May God bless and keep you!

To Coach Bea, You are my Aaron. Moses didn't believe he could fulfill God's mission had God not sent him some help. Sometimes, we just need a little push. I'm so grateful for your love, prayers and support because without none of this would be possible. Love you to LIFE!!!

To everyone who reads this, I pray this book will be food to your soul. Kingdom building means Kingdom living! GOD BLESS!!!

In Christ,
    Chesma M

OVERCOMER:

To get the better result of in a struggle or conflict; conquer; defeat: to overcome the enemy, prevail over or triumph

(Retrieved from https://www.dictionary.com/browse/overcomer)

D^{AY 1}

I AM Beautiful

I WILL PRAISE THEE; for I am fearfully and wonderfully made: marvelous are thy works; and that my soul knoweth right well. (Psalms 139:14)

I AM beautiful because I know my worth and in spite of my flaws, I'm not afraid to shine through them anyway. I am beautiful because I love to see the beauty in others just as God sees the best in me. I am beautiful because even when I'm discouraged, I can still feel God's presence from within. Beauty is not about fashion models and keeping up with the latest trends. Beauty is way more than skin deep. Because real beauty lies through the Eyes of the Beholder!

I remember growing up as a child being ridiculed because of my dark skin. I was never recognized as the popular girl in school nor did I ever have a boyfriend. Now I did have a crush but when he found out I liked him; he laughed at me, called me ugly and ran away from me. I felt so ashamed because it wasn't of mutual consent. I was so heartbroken that I started to believe the lies and I began transforming myself into what I thought beauty was supposed to look like.

I'm so grateful that God doesn't judge my outside appearance! He is more concerned about what's on the inside. Many disappointments have taught me how to embrace my scars so each scar can tell a story. My smile, personality, and character all reflect the beauty of His grace. I shall give Him all the praise and glory due His Name. Amen.

1. **I AM Beautiful**

Look not on his countenance, or on height of his stature; because I have refused him: for the Lord seeth not as man looketh on the outward appearance, but the Lord looketh on the heart. (1 Samuel 16:7)

D^{AY 2}

I AM Strong

*A*ND HE SAID UNTO ME, *'My grace is sufficient for thee: for my strength is made perfect in weakness.'* (2 Corinthians 12:9)

I AM strong because I know what it feels like to feel pain and despite everything that I've been through I'm still here. I am strong because it helps me to lift others up when they're down. I am strong because I am dependent on God!

I've learned having strength doesn't always mean you're dependent upon self but you're able to fully rely on God's power whenever you fall short of His glory! I was reminded that I cannot depend on my own strength. My experiences have always taught me that it's ok to be vulnerable because I can trust that His strength will always be greater than my weakness.

It wasn't until I lost my job that LIFE's circumstances began to shift. And even in His infinite wisdom, He allowed for things to happen because He has greater plans for me. But I never lost my praise! It is often when one door closes God will open another because His rejection is for our own protection.

No matter how many times I fell down, God was always there to pick me up. It's comforting to know that despite my failures God's grace was always sufficient. I am grateful that the God I serve is more than enough! The test of true faith is how to remain humble in the face of adversity; for I am weak, He is strong!

2. **I AM Strong**

Come unto me, all ye that labour and heavy laden, and I will give you rest. (Matthew 11:28)

D^{AY 3}

SHINE BRIGHT Like a Diamond

AND BE NOT CONFORMED to this world: but be ye transformed by the renewing of your mind, that ye may prove what is that good and acceptable, and perfect, will of God. (Romans 12:2)

I AM valuable because I'm unique and there's none like me. He made me unique because my assignment is specific. It was never meant for me to fit in because I was born to stand out. My LIFE and family are blessed by each contribution that I make. I am valuable because I am God's asset!

I was bought with a price and because I am a servant of God it is imperative that I walk upright and worthy of His calling. It sets the stage for an abundance of blessings and if I'm faithful and yet obedient I will allow my blessings to manifest and make room for overflow. But sometimes I tend to get in my own way.

IT WAS prom night of my senior year and I learned that a group of my classmates were throwing an after party at a hotel to have some drinks so I went to join in for the fun. I knew it wasn't the right thing to do but popularity and peer pressure played major influences throughout my high school career and I knew if I wanted to be a part of the in-crowd, I had to make the ultimate sacrifice. But there are consequences for every action.

I was reminded to be an example just like Jesus because purpose will always be bigger than any popularity contest that can ever compare. Because everybody wants to be a diamond until they find out what it costs to be cut. Thank God that His grace allows room for mistakes. I'm blessed to know God still calls me His own!

3. **Shine Bright Like a Diamond**

You were bought with a price; be not ye servants of men. (1 Corinthians 7:23)

D^{AY 4}

Jesus Loves ME

FOR GOD so loved the world, that he gave his only begotten Son, that whosoever believeth in him should not perish but have everlasting life. (John 3:16)

I AM LOVED because I could not experience an abundant LIFE without Jesus and the cross. I am alive because of who He is in me. He loved me beyond my faults. It is by grace that I am saved by my faith. God's love teaches me to meet people where they are. Because His love is unconditional.

I am loved because I am a believer in Christ. There is no specialized skills test that you have to pass nor is it rocket science. All you have to do is BELIEVE! I accepted Jesus as my Saviour at age fourteen and I didn't understand what my purpose was until I matured spiritually. All of my LIFE's experiences have taught me that having been saved does not exempt me from trials and error but God's grace is a security key to eternal freedom. I live to share my testimony with everyone I meet.

It wasn't until I worked at the mall as a shampoo technician that I learned that one of my coworkers restored her LIFE to Christ because of my influence. We all need to be mindful how we live because we may be the only Bible that someone reads.

If we say we are Christians and live like we're not then how can we convince them that God is who He says He is? Because His grace was made available to all so we shall give it freely to others. Yet, the same grace that saved me can save someone else. I am grateful to be alive because of His love.

4. Jesus Loves ME

Let your light so shine before men, that they may see your good works, and glorify your Father which is in heaven. (Matthew 5:16)

D^{AY} 5

I AM FORGIVEN

FOR ALL HAVE SINNED and fallen short of the glory of God. (Romans 3:23)

I'M like a tree with leaves that have fallen by the wayside. The key to bearing fruit is to meditate on God's word day and night. If I don't stand firmly in my faith, I won't stand at all. But the Truth shall make me FREE!!!

I plant a seed to secure a harvest of a sure foundation. My foundation is deeply rooted in Jesus so that I can make Him my priority and if I shall stumble He lifts me up. When I suffered a miscarriage, I fell into despair and begin to search outside of God's will for comfort; however, He is faithful and made a way for me to resist temptation.

Sometimes when you spend enough time in the dark, you will learn how to appreciate the light. I was tired of feeling the hurt, guilt, and shame. I found joy in the comfort of having dead weight lifted off my shoulders.

Forgiveness is freedom of God's power and love. When you learn to let go and trust in Him, you will go from a victim to victorious. I am no longer defeated by my past. Because my soul says YES to God; a total surrender!

5. **I AM Forgiven**

There hath no temptation taken you but such as is common to man: but God is faithful, who will not suffer you to be tempted above that ye are able; but will with that temptation also make a way to escape, that ye may be able to bear it. (1 Corinthians 10:13)

D^{AY 6}

BE Fearless

> *Now unto him that is able to do exceedingly abundantly above all that we ask or think, according to the power that worketh in us, Unto him be the glory in the church by Christ Jesus throughout all ages, world without end. Amen. (Ephesians 3:20-21)*

GOD IS able to do immeasurably more in my LIFE than I can ever imagine. I can approach Him with freedom and confidence through faith in Jesus. The power of God works through me as I affirm that it's His treasure inside this jar of clay.

The purpose that God has for me is greater than I can obtain. There's no reason to fear because I've been equipped with everything that I need to fulfill His will. And, sometimes He will make you do things outside your comfort zone.

I've always had a fear of the public platform because I feared rejection. But sometimes God will send someone or even place you in a position to do things above the influence. I felt like Moses. He was led by Aaron. He was a man of faith who murmured and muttered when he talked but ended up dividing and conquering the land to free the people from bondage. God told him in Exodus to go tell Pharaoh to let the people go. He also delivered the Ten Commandments, parted the Red Sea, and led the Israelites to the Promised Land.

And just like Moses, I want to be great. This reminded me to always take courage and never fear. Because the task ahead of you will never be as great as the power behind you. I finally found my strength and belief in Him; this gives me peace. I am fearless because God is ABLE!

6. **BE Fearless**

Finally, my brethren, be strong in the Lord, and in the power of his might. Put on the whole armour of God, that ye may be able to stand against the wiles of the devil. (Ephesians 6:10)

D^{AY} 7

My Soul Has Been Anchored

But the anointing which ye have received of him abideth in you, and ye need not that any man teach you: but as the same anointing teacheth you of all things, and is truth, and is no lie, and even as it hath taught you, ye shall abide in him. (1 John 2:27)

God has equipped me with everything I need to pursue my purpose. I don't need anyone's permission nor do I need their validation to do what he has called of me. As long as I stand on His word, no obstacle can defeat me because my mind is programmed for victory!

When God has called you, nobody can interrupt the plans that He has for you. Touch not my anointed. You don't need any title, degrees or special certificates to qualify you to do the work of the Lord, ALL you need is the Holy Spirit. Let God be your vindicator and He will protect you from the evil one.

NOBODY'S TASK will be the same so run your own race. No matter the storm that you face, don't get distracted and stay the course. Remember, God calms ALL winds! You may not understand the plan that He has for you, just look to the hills because that's where your help comes from.

7. **My Soul Has Been Anchored**

Do not touch my anointed and do my prophets any harm. (Psalms 105:15)

D*AY 8*

KNOW YOUR WORTH

*A*ND LET *the beauty of the LORD our God be upon us: and establish thou the work of our hands upon us; yea, the work of our hands establish thou it. (Psalms 90:17)*

I AM worthy of His freedom, grace and unending compassion. I am worthy enough to follow my dreams and manifest my desires. I am worthy enough to know that if I am tired that I can find rest in God! All of my battles are His that if I stand firm in faith, He fights for me.

I'm so grateful that God doesn't treat us as our sins deserve. His grace allows us room for mistakes. Sometimes we base our lives off statistics of what we've seen and heard. We often get distracted by what we desire instead of God's divine promise. But I've learned that LIFE is not about what we want but in what we give. It is His destiny that has designed us into how we live.

STOP OVERWORKING yourself for a position that was promised to someone else. No one will ever treat you the way you deserve like God. Because what He has for you is for you. Favor will place you in a position that accolades won't. Remember, God doesn't call the qualified, but instead He qualifies the called.

When I graduated college, I hoped to get a job in my career of accounting. I worked at a marketing firm for two years before I got laid off and even worked some temporary assignments in between. It took five years before I got a permanent job and still not in my background, but God's favor proved that He would keep me in position to do what He desires.

I've learned that you don't need any degree or diploma to prove that you're worthy of serving the kingdom. Just be who He created you to be because you're deserving and oh so worthy!

8. **KNOW YOUR WORTH**

Let love and faithfulness never leave you; bind them around your neck, write them on the tablet in your heart, then you will win favor and a good name in the sight of God and man. (Proverbs 3:3-4)

D^{AY 9}

I AM Chosen

CREATE in me a clean heart and renew a right spirit within me. (Psalms 51:10)

I AM CREATED in God's image. I am one of His own. I am chosen and appointed by Christ to bear His fruit. God has chosen me to be in His kingdom so that I may have tremendous significance. Because many are called, but a few are chosen.

I'm like a rose that has been withered away but God handpicked me specifically from His garden and designed for His purpose. A rose doesn't worry about being a flower nor does it compete for attention because every rose has thorns. It just blooms right where it's planted.

When I was younger, I was always picked last and never got to play on the A-team in high school so I felt like a loser. I thought being picked by the A-team meant being picked by the best. But I didn't realize that being picked by God I was already chosen by the best.

I was reminded that I may not be their pick because I'm God's chosen. Never settle for less when you have been chosen by the best. Not only have I been set apart but I've been chosen and created for serving a great purpose.

9. **I AM Chosen**

So, the last will be first, and the first last: for many be called, but few chosen. (Matthew 20:16)

D^{AY 10}

LIVE ON PURPOSE

AND WE KNOW that all things work together for good to them that love God, to them who are called according to his purpose. (Romans 8:28 KJV)

I LOOK into God's perfect law and am blessed to do what it says. He has equipped me perfectly through Jesus to do certain things which I am now doing. I love God with my whole heart because I work to honor Him. I am a woman of true purpose, courage and strength.

I have been destined to serve my purpose. It's mine and nobody can take it away from me. I live only to serve Him. It's not about having talent or skill but about carrying out God's will.

Purpose isn't something you run from but rather to. It will help keep you aligned with God. It also helps you create opportunities for yourself and others. Your purpose is unique and specific. Nobody

will have the same task as you were given. Make your
purpose your passion.

10. **LIVE ON PURPOSE**

*For I know the plans that I have for you, said the Lord,
thoughts of peace, not of evil, to give you an expected end.*
(Jeremiah 29:11)

D AY II

BE A Blessing

> *Neither do men light a candle, and put it under a bushel,*
> *but on a candlestick; and it giveth light unto all that are*
> *in the house. Let your light so shine before men, that they*
> *may see your good works, and glorify your Father which*
> *is in heaven. (Matthew 5:15-16)*

I AM A LIVING TESTIMONY. It is important how I live because I am a reflection of God's grace. I am content in His sufficiency and I don't hoard over my blessings. The windows of Heaven pour out more than I can receive. The overflow is not so we can have room enough to store but so we can share plenty with others. I don't hide my light under a basket. I let it shine for all to see so everyone will praise my Father.

There are many ways to share in service and give to others in need. We just have to create the opportunity to do so because the person that we might be entertaining could be an angel in disguise.

When my husband and I go out on date nights we

would request to-go trays to give to the homeless and create hygiene bags to pass out to them on the street corner and we also adopted a family during the holidays.

It's a blessing to share with others of what God has done for me because it's a blessing to give than to receive. I am blessed to be a blessing!

11. **BE A Blessing**

I have shewed you all things, how that so laboring ye ought to support the weak, and to remember the words of the Lord Jesus, how he said, it more blessed to give than receive. (Acts 20:35)

D^{AY 12}

MY NAME IS Victory

YE ARE OF GOD, little children, and have overcome them: because greater is he that is in you, than he that is in the world. (1 John 4:4)

GOD'S SPIRIT in me is greater than any other spirit in the world. He enables me to live a victorious LIFE. I speak LIFE over my fears and my doubts. I will not be defeated in my mind or in my LIFE. I am more than a conqueror in God!

I was inspired by Gospel songwriter, Jonathan Nelson's song, "My Name Is Victory." Because when you know who you are in Christ you have nothing to fear. There is no room for competition because I have already been declared a winner in Jesus. The mistakes I've made can't even be compared to the beauty of His grace. Tell the devil he is defeated!

I remember playing volleyball in middle school; when we prayed before our games God would always shift them in our favor. Because the power of prayer moves the hand of God. This reminded me to remain steadfast in Him to be able to stand against the opponent.

Don't worry about those who told you what you can't do, JUST do what God has created you to do. Because when you learn to depend on God's power you can WIN!!!

12. **My Name Is Victory**

And David girded his sword upon his armour, and he assayed to go; for he had not proved it. And David said to Saul, I cannot go with these; for I have not proved them. And David put them off him. (1 Samuel 17:39)

D^{AY 13}

I Choose Joy

A joyful heart is good medicine, but a crushed spirit dries up the bones. (Proverbs 17:22 ESV)

I choose joy. I am shaking off any guilt or shame and living in the right now because the joy of the Lord is my strength. I have great joy because I obey God's commands and remain in His love. Having such joy is God's unshakeable confidence!

There is a difference between joy and happiness. Happiness is contingent upon LIFE's happenings; while joy is the beauty of God's grace! No matter my circumstance I choose to shift my perspective. I take full control of my LIFE and destiny. I avoid any negativity and drama that comes my way because unlike misery, she loves company and I refuse to accept her invitation. Because joy is a gift from God and nobody can take it away!

There were many times in my LIFE where I was involved in an altercation with my peers. I now realize that at the end of the day everyone has a right to their opinion. I've learned that not everything deserves a response. But you have to know how to choose your own battles. Let God be your vindicator!

A valuable lesson in this is to never allow anyone to make you become so bitter that you lose yourself in the process. Nobody holds that much power. It's not anyone's decision to choose what's best for you. You are responsible for your own actions and how you respond is up to you. Today, I CHOOSE JOY!

13. **I Choose Joy**

And the peace of God, which passeth all understanding, shall keep your hearts and minds through Christ Jesus. (Philippians 4:7)

D AY 14

STIR Up Your Gifts

LET every skillful craftsman among you come and make all that Lord has commanded. (Exodus 35:10)

I AM GIFTED because God created me for the purpose of serving others. God's glory is greater than my gift and He is faithful. He'll complete the work that he has begun in me and my gifts will make room for me. I am able to share my gifts with honor and pleasure. All of my gifts are for His Glory!

We stir up our gifts through Godly discipline, which produces the fruit of God's nature in our lives. There is a difference between spiritual gifts and talents but both are gifts from God. And, both are given for the purpose of serving others.

The purpose of serving others is to glorify God while encouraging, edifying and empowering the church. He wants us to use our gifts He has given us to impact the lost by bringing them into the Kingdom. I have been given the gift of service and its

uniqueness to empower the church and community.
Pastors' Closet was created for this purpose. Stir up
the gifts within you by the power of the Holy Spirit!

14. **Stir Up Your Gifts**

*Wherefore I put thee I remembrance that thou stir up
the gift of God, which is in thee by putting on of my hands.*
(1Timothy 1:6-7)

D^{AY 15}

ORDER My Steps

LET NOT mercy and truth forsake thee: bind them about thy neck; write them upon a table of thine heart. (Proverbs 3:3)

I AM who I am because Christ lives in me. I do not worry about LIFE's happenings and I have nothing to fear. All of my LIFE's challenges have led me closer to God. I depend on His guidance that comforts me. I'm equipped and aligned with my purpose.

Because I have written love and faithfulness on the tablet of my heart, I have favor with God. I can find all the answers I need for my LIFE from within; they are in my deep subconscious and wait for me to explore. I go within, answer a question, have patience and trust, the answer will come to me through the wisdom of God's mercy and truth.

The work of my hands and the plans of my LIFE are now moving quickly towards a sure and perfect fulfillment. I anticipate the good in God's right action, I now place my full trust. This is a time of divine completion. I now reap a harvest of good as miracles follow miracles, and wonders never cease. My steps have been ordered!

15. **Order My Steps**

Being confident of this very thing, that he hath begun a good work in you will perform it until the day of Jesus Christ. (Philippians 1:6)

D^{AY 16}

GROW in Faith

BE CAREFUL FOR NOTHING; but in everything by prayer and supplication with thanksgiving let your requests be known to God. And the peace of God, which passeth all understanding, shall keep your hearts and minds through Christ Jesus. (Philippians 4:6-7)

A PLANT CANNOT GROW and thrive if it's not planted in the right soil. If I'm not rooted in Christ, being nourished by His word then I'm literally wilting from the inside out. Death is imminent if I am not rooted and built up in Christ.

When I humble myself before God in prayer, He hears me and I gain understanding. My negative feelings don't come from Him so I don't have to put up with them. I give all my anxieties to Him and know that He'll take them because He loves me. This gives me peace, hope and serenity. Therefore, I shall walk in faithfulness. I walk in obedience. I walk in care. I walk in dependability. I walk in piety. I walk in truth. God's word is truth. I grow in faith!

16. **Grow in Faith**

Cast all your burdens upon the Lord, and he shall sustain thee: he shall never suffer the righteous to be moved. (Psalms 55:22)

DAY 17

BE Inspired

Oh, how I love thy law! It is my meditation all the day.
(Psalms 119:97)

I LOVE God's principles and meditate on them day and night. I have a sound mind full of good thoughts, not of defeat. They guide me in the right direction. By faith, I am well able. I am equipped. I am anointed. I am empowered. My steps are ordered!

I manifest my desires. I have overcome my fears. I refuse to give up until I have exhausted all my options. I have become more inspired and empowered every day. I don't depend on anyone else's quotes of wisdom but instead I look to God for direction to get me through.

God's word challenges me to be greater than myself. I rely on His strength to help me to move forward in my daily walk. Today I bless my being with limitless inspiration. My inspiration comes from God alone!

17. **BE Inspired**

All scripture is given by inspiration by God and is profitable for teaching, for rebuking, for correcting, for training in righteousness. (2 Timothy 3:16)

D^{AY 18}

I WALK In Humility

LET nothing be done through strife or vainglory; but in lowliness of mind let each esteem other better than themselves. (Philippians 2:3)

I AM humble enough to know that I'm not better than anybody but I'm also wise enough to know that I am different from the rest. I am humble enough to seek help when I need it. I choose to be humble because I know that I deserve it.

I am content in my circumstances. I don't want for anything because the God I serve is more than enough. I give freely without reward. I don't have all the answers as I continue to learn new things every day.

When I make mistakes, I can always depend on God's strength to correct the err of my ways. Sometimes it's hard to stand out from the crowd but He reminds me that I'm different from the rest. I am humble enough to realize that I cannot do this alone.

I've learned what I go through, I also can grow through. I walk in humility.

18. **I Walk In Humility**

I therefore, the prisoner of the Lord, beseech you brethren to walk worthy of your calling with lowliness and meekness, with longsuffering, forbearing one another in love. (Ephesians 4:1, 2)

D^{AY 19}

BE Grateful

O GIVE *thanks unto the Lord; for he is good: for his mercy endureth for ever. (Psalm 136:1)*

GRATEFULNESS IS A PREREQUISITE TO HAPPINESS. It sets the stage for abundance. When what I have is enough, I've become content and open to receiving more. Gratitude makes sense of our past, brings peace for today, and creates a vision for tomorrow.

Gratitude grounds me in my faith. It teaches me to grow in spirit and truth. I'm thankful for new beginnings. There are times that I have felt overwhelmed but God reminds me of my worth. God looks beyond my faults and supports my desires.

No matter my circumstance there's always something to be grateful for. LIFE gives me an abundance of blessings to be grateful for. Having an attitude of gratitude is the key to manifesting a better LIFE for myself. I am eternally grateful!

19. **BE Grateful**

I am not saying this because I am in need, for I have learned to be in content whatever the circumstance. (Philippians 4:11)

D^{AY 20}

GOD FAVORS ME

AND GOD IS able to make all grace abound toward you; that ye, always having all sufficiency in all things, may abound to every good work. (2 Corinthians 9:8)

I DECLARE I am grateful for who God is in my LIFE and for what He's done. I will not take for granted the people and opportunities, and the favor He blessed me with. I will walk in humility and integrity. My heart will overflow with praise and gratitude for all His goodness and mercy.

God's favor brought me from a lot of dark places. He was there for my protection. He protects me in my home, on my job, traveling down the dangerous highways and even from my enemies. He kept me out of trouble and away from danger.

Sometimes LIFE's experiences will challenge you to begin to question God but His favor has opened up many opportunities I didn't even qualify for. I remember applying for my first job as a cashier at a

burger stand that just opened up; although I had no
experience but God saw fit to shift things in my
favor. It is by faith that He is the only reason I've
made it this far. Because God favors me!

20. **GOD Favors Me**

*The favor of God rests on me and His wisdom
strengthens inner man.* (Numbers 6:24-26)

D^{AY 21}

I AM A SERVANT

FOR DO I now persuade men, or God? Or do I seek to please men? For if I yet pleased men, I should not be a servant of Christ. (Galatians 1:10)

I AM ENOUGH. I let go of what is not serving me, and accept who I am today. I am fulfilled by serving my LIFE's purposes. My service puts me in submission with God; giving Him all the glory and honor He is due. I will serve Him with my whole heart!

I am equipped to conquer all of LIFE's challenges. I choose to let go of everything that doesn't serve me. I am divinely guided in all I do. I am thankful for the abundance I have in my LIFE. I am aligned with God's will and purpose.

I've been called by every name except a Child of God so I ignore my critics. I serve with purpose. I serve with grace. I serve with love. I'm not here to make friends. I'm only here to WIN SOULS! God is the only one that I aimed to please and at the end of the day the seven words that I want to hear are, "Well done, my good and faithful servant."

21. **I AM a Servant**

His Lord said unto him, Well done, thou good and faithful servant: thou hast been faithful over a few things, I will make thee ruler over many things: enter thou into the joy of thy Lord. (Matthew 25:21)

D^{AY 22}

I AM BUILT For This

FOR I KNOW the thoughts that I think toward you, saith the Lord, thoughts of peace, and not of evil, to give you an expected ending. (Jeremiah 29:11)

IT IS NOT TOO late to accomplish everything God has placed in my heart. I have not missed my window of opportunity. God has moments of favor in my future. He is preparing me for right now because He is releasing a special grace to help me accomplish my dream. This is my time. This is my moment. For I have been created for a time such as this!

God has laid my LIFE out on a blueprint. He is releasing favor into my LIFE right now. He has ordered my steps. Nobody can interrupt the plans that He has for my LIFE because I have been given all the necessary tools that I need to fulfill my purpose. I have been assigned to this mountain to show others that it can be moved. I have not been given a specific date to complete my assignment. In due time I will pursue the mission that God has prepared for me. I Am Built For This!

22. **I AM Built For This**

For if thou altogether holdest thy peace at this time, then shall there enlargement and deliverance arise to the Jews from another place; but thou and thy father's house shall be destroyed: and who knoweth whether thou art come to the kingdom for such a time as this? (Esther 4:14)

D^{AY 23}

BE ENCOURAGED

MY BRETHREN, count it all joy when ye fall into divers temptations. Knowing this, that the trying of your faith worketh patience. (James 1:2-3)

EVERYDAY WON'T FEEL like Sunday. I will speak LIFE over my trials and tribulations. I will not allow negative thoughts to consume my mind. Let the joy overrule in my heart. The joy of the Lord is my strength. This too shall pass.

Don't just praise God in the sunshine but also learn how to dance in the rain. For, it is within our deepest pain that we will soon discover His divine plan. It gives birth to our destiny. God is working on us for a specific purpose.

Nothing has ever caught Him by surprise. No matter what you face today know that He will make a way out of no way because He loves you and will see you through. Be encouraged today because God always finishes what He started!

23. **BE Encouraged**

For His anger endureth but a moment; in his favour is life: weeping may endure for a night, but joy cometh in the morning. (Psalms 30:5)

D^{AY 24}

I AM An Overcomer

Not as though I had already attained, either were already perfect: but I follow after, if that I may apprehend that for which also, I am apprehended in Christ Jesus. Brethren, I do not count myself to have apprehended: but this one thing that I do, forgetting those which are behind, and reaching forth unto those which are before, I press toward the mark for the prize of the high calling of God in Christ Jesus. (Philippians 3:12-14)

I AM AN OVERCOMER. I am committed to the call and dedicated to living out holiness in my everyday LIFE. I am reborn with a new orientation and new expectation. Each day I rise expecting the impossible because God gives me the power to resist and strength to endure. This is my purpose.

I am not perfect by any means. I am a child of God and cannot be defeated. There have been many weapons that have formed but didn't prosper. I have overcome many challenges of defeat: adversity, temptation, rejection and depression BUT God delivered me from them all.

I speak LIFE over my circumstances and it has taught me how to be humble in spite of everything. What didn't kill me has definitely made me stronger. My faith is my weapon that puts me in a position of purpose. Because God is right there with me. I Am More Than A Conqueror! I'm An OVERCOMER!

24. I AM An Overcomer

Be strong and courageous. Do not fear or be in dread of them, for it is the Lord your God who goes with you. He will never leave you nor forsake you. (Deuteronomy 31:6)

D^{AY 25}

I SHALL NOT WANT

But seek ye first the kingdom of God, and his righteousness; and all these things shall be added unto you. Take therefore no thought for the morrow: for the morrow shall take thought for the things of itself. Sufficient unto the day is evil thereof. (Matthew 6:33-34)

MY GOD IS rich in houses and land. I don't worry about everyday LIFE. I will not chase after money and material things; I will attract it. God knows my needs and meets them because I make his kingdom my primary concern. He is my provider and my supplier of all things – Jehovah Jireh!

There's nothing I need in this world that I can't go to ask my Father. I have food, clothing and shelter. I do not seek after fame or fortune because He is the owner of all things. God is my protector. He is my security. He is my keeper. I shall not want for nothing!

25. **I Shall Not Want**

Let not your heart be troubled: ye believe in God, believe also me. In my Father's house are many mansions: if it were not so, I would have told you. I go to prepare a place for you. (John 14:1-2)

D AY 26

FOLLOW Your Heart

KEEP thy heart with all diligence; for out of it are the issues of life. (Proverbs 4:23)

I HAVE DISCERNMENT. I can see the big picture and make wise decisions to look at the paths before me. I have a sense of what feels right or wrong and use discernment when making choices about my companions and surroundings. I walk with God wherever I go!

There is no dream too big or too small; you can be anything that you want to be. No matter what you do, you will always be surrounded by critics. What's impossible for man is possible for God. Don't let the noise of the world disrupt the plans that God has in store for your LIFE! Trust God, believe in yourself and all your plans will succeed. Follow your heart!

26. **Follow Your Heart**

Trust in the Lord with all thine heart; and lean not unto thine own understanding. In all thy ways acknowledge Him and He shall direct thy paths. (Proverbs 3:5-6)

D^{AY 27}

BE TRANSFORMED

THEREFORE, if any man be in Christ, he is a new creature: old things are passed away; behold, all things become new. (2 Corinthians 5:17)

I HAVE the grace that I need for today. I put on my garment of praise. The places I used to go, I don't go anymore. I will walk boldly with confidence in His strength and power. Nothing I face will be too hard for me to conquer. I declare that I am His and He is mine. I am His masterpiece.

God made dirt and dirt won't hurt. Everything that we go through we must GROW through. Sometimes when God wants us to move, He makes us uncomfortable. Just as the caterpillar transforms into the butterfly, so do we. Stop living in the garden of comfort because nothing grows there.

As the American essayist, Ralph Waldo Emerson said it best, "Sorrow looks back, worry looks around and FAITH looks up." Therefore I'm no longer looking back at my past, I'm looking ahead.

BE Transformed!

27. **BE Transformed**

That if thou shalt confess with thy mouth the Lord Jesus, and shalt believe in thine heart that God hath raised him from the dead, thou shalt be saved. (Romans 10:9)

D^{AY 28}

BE The Miracle

NOT OF WORKS, lest any man should boast. For we his workmanship, created in Christ Jesus unto good works, which God hath before ordained that we should walk in them. (Ephesians 2:9-10)

I AM HIS MASTERPIECE. I am above average. The grace that I have, I didn't earn and I don't deserve it. All that I am I owe it all to Him. My shield and faith comfort me. I walk in His example of humility.

One of my favorite movies is "Bruce Almighty" starring Jim Carrey and Morgan Freeman. God tells Bruce that the problem with everybody is they're too busy looking up when they should be looking from within.

Everything that we have God has given us power to do for ourselves. Stop waiting for an opportunity and go out and create it yourself. Find whatever you're passionate about and use it to help serve the community to make a difference.

You are the miracle.

BE The Miracle!

28. **BE The Miracle**

What doth it profit, my brethren, though a man say he hath faith, and have not works? Can faith save him? If a brother or sister be naked and destitute of daily food, And you say to them, Depart in peace, notwithstanding ye give not those things, which are needful to the body. What doth it profit? Even so faith, if it hath not works, is dead, being alone. (James 2:14-17)

D AY 29

I AM Delivered

For if, when we were enemies, we were reconciled to God by the death of His Son, much more, being reconciled, we shall be saved by His life. (Romans 5:10)

I AM REDEEMED, and I am saying so. The blood of Jesus cleanses me from all sickness, disease and poverty. I am renewed by the strength of His power. I have the blessings that overrides all the curses of the Earth. He is the full and final payment for all my past, present and future sins, failures and shortcomings. I have total dependence on Him alone.

I've gone through a lot of things, seen many places and experienced both seen and unseen danger. I don't go to the places that I used to. I don't hang out with the people that I used to. I don't do the things that I used to. Thank God, that I don't look like what I've been through. I surround myself with those who help keep me accountable. I Am Delivered!

29. **I AM Delivered**

I have been young, and now am old; yet have I not seen the righteous forsaken, nor his seed begging bread. (Psalms 37:25)

D^{AY 30}

I AM ENOUGH

I WILL LIFT up mine eyes unto the hills, from whence cometh my help. My help cometh from the Lord, which made heaven and earth. (Psalms 121:1-2)

I AM EQUIPPED for every good work God has planned out for me. I am anointed and empowered to be all that He created me to be. There are things that I don't understand right now but I allow Him to be my guide. There is nothing that I cannot do because I put my trust in Him. My steps are ordered.

I don't worry about feeling unappreciated because I am full of LIFE with endless possibilities. I don't look for anyone to validate me because I've been called by God alone.

I am worthy. I am loved. I am good enough. I have enough. I AM Enough!

30. **I AM Enough**

I can do all things through Christ which strengtheneth me.
(Philippians 4:13)

D^{AY 31}

I AM Kingdom

JESUS SAITH UNTO HIM, 'I am the way, the truth, and the life: no man cometh unto the Father, but by me.' (John 14:6)

I AM with God and He is with me. I can see the kingdom because I am born again. I am divinely connected and in alignment with my purpose. This Earth is not my home, for the Kingdom is my goal! Someday I'll be in heaven with my Father because I know the way there through Jesus!

I grew up in the foster system so I felt alone. I thought my whole world was crashing down. I became so afraid. My childhood was a big blur so I didn't have any memories to reminisce on. The family that I once knew had been taken from me. I thought about running away but God had ordered my steps.

Family may not always be blood, but having people around you to love you past your pain. It will help fill your void. I do not fret about shattered beginnings because I know that's not how my story ends. Everything that is attached to Him belongs to me and I'm rich in all things.

I've learned that whenever you find yourself in unfamiliar territory you can always seek to ask Him to be your guide. Having His grace has taught me to remain humble in spite of my circumstances. The bridge over troubled waters is through Jesus, because He kept me in the midst of it all! I AM Kingdom!!!

31. **I AM Kingdom**

"Bridge over troubled waters" by Simon & Garfunkel

ABOUT THE AUTHOR

Chesma Comer McCoy was born in Austin, TX to Arnold M. Comer, Jr. and Gayle Marshall Comer on September 11, 1981. She is the youngest of three daughters, Vanessa Hardison, (Killeen, TX) and Valancia Comer, (Austin, TX).

She was placed in the foster care system at the tender age of 3 and raised by her legal guardians James and Girtie Crathers of Bartlett, TX for 15 years. They have a family of 11 and a host of grandchildren and great-grandchildren.

She is a firm believer of Our Lord and Saviour, Jesus Christ and was saved at the age of 14 years old at Holy Temple COGIC, Pastor Langston B. Williams, Sr., Bartlett, TX.

She graduated high school at Bartlett High School in May 2000 and moved back to Austin, TX to reunite with her mother.

She served as a choir member and on the junior missions ministry at Rosewood Baptist Church, Coby Shorter, III, Pastor in November 2000.

She is married to Leonard McCoy of 16 years, (January 24, 2004) and a mother of two children, Cheston and Leandra McCoy.

She went into depression after she suffered a miscarriage of their second child and lost her job in September 2009, which later caused their separation that led to divorce BUT by the Grace of God, they reunited in March 2014.

She reinstated her LIFE back to Christ and was baptized in November 2015 by Pastor Eric Jones of Emmanuel Bible-The Love Church, Austin, TX.

She is now a dedicated and faithful servant of the Abundant LIFE Community Baptist Church of Pflugerville, TX, where DeChard I.H.M. Freeman is Pastor. (March 2016)

She has obtained her LIFE Coach certification, Pastor Connie Stewart, Believer's Empowerment Church and Owner and CEO of Bloom U of Houston, TX in November 2018.

She founded Pastors' Closet a 501(c)(3) non-profit organization in November 2018 as an extension of her service.

Her services will include prayer, daily devotions, wellness conferences, spiritual retreats, coaching, outreach, support services to all Christian leaders in need all a part of faith- based and biblical principles.

She expresses her love and compassion to each pastor for the love and dedication they all bring to the church and community.

Her purpose and passion for pursuing this mission is dedicated to the pastors who lost their lives to suicide and depression. She pays homage and tribute by serving in love and humility. She is dedicated to this purpose and strives each new day as God gives her strength.

Her favorite scripture is Psalms 121 and her favorite hymn is "I Love to Praise Him" Donnie McClurkin's version.

CPSIA information can be obtained
at www.ICGtesting.com
Printed in the USA
FSHW020959110521
81233FS